The Robot Meets a Tiger

Written by Becca Heddle

Illustrated by Amerigo Pinelli

Collins

I feel awake and fine! Full of power.
Time to get going.

I am entering a new zone. Its name is "outside". This field is made of concrete.

A new thing is sprawling across the concrete. It has paws. It is alive!

It has fine fur with stripes.

Computer!
What is this beast?

6

The tiger is waking up. Its jaws open wide in a yawn.

Its mouth is full of teeth like spikes. Will it bite me with those teeth?

It's time to put up my shields!
They will protect me.

But a paw traps me. No! This is not safe.
I must get away.

Sharp claws shoot out of the tiger's paw.
They make a grating sound.

My lasers zap the tiger.
But the tiger is not exploding.

Zap!

I am shaking. I must control my fear to get home.

I have a plan.

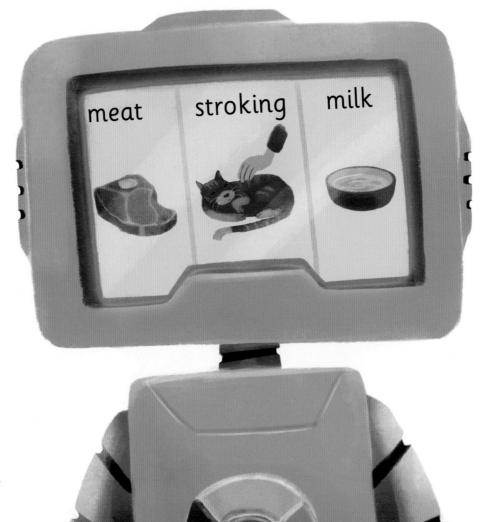

I stroke the tiger. The claws retreat. The tiger gazes at me.

The tiger is not smiling.

It takes me in its jaws.

Don't chew me!

I poke it and squirm.

It will not let me go.

I cannot escape these teeth.
The tiger is taking me away.

Later ... This is my base! I rode home in the tiger's mouth!

Robot's day outside